## THE STORY BEHIND

# RUBBER

Barbara A. Somervill

**Heinemann Library**
**Chicago, Illinois**

**www.heinemannraintree.com**
Visit our website to find out
more information about
Heinemann-Raintree books.

**To order:**
☎ Phone 888-454-2279
💻 Visit www.heinemannraintree.com
to browse our catalog and order online.

Edited by Megan Cotugno and Diyan Leake
Designed by Philippa Jenkins
Original illustrations © Capstone Global Library Ltd.
Illustrated by Oxford Designers and Illustrators
Picture research by Hannah Taylor and Mica Brancic
Production by Eirian Griffiths
Originated by Capstone Global Library
Printed in China by CTPS

15 14 13 12 11
10 9 8 7 6 5 4 3 2 1

**Library of Congress Cataloging-in-Publication Data**
Somervill, Barbara A.
  The story behind rubber / Barbara A. Somervill.
    p. cm.—(True stories)
  Includes bibliographical references and index.
  ISBN 978-1-4329-5439-0 (hc)
  I. Title.
  TA455.R8S66 2012
  678'.2—dc22          2010042104

**Acknowledgments**
The author and publishers are grateful to the following for
permission to reproduce copyright material:
Alamy Images p. 24 (© Dennis MacDonald); Corbis pp.
11 (ClassicStock/ H. Armstrong Roberts), 25 (Roger
Tidman), 9 (© Bettmann); Getty Images pp. 12 (Time
Life Pictures/ Gordon Coster), 17 (Bloomberg/ Dario
Pignatelli), 20 (Photographer's Choice/David Madison);
istockphoto p. 7 (© Steven Wynn); Photolibrary p. 21
(Image100); Shutterstock pp. 4 (© Adrian Hughes), 5
(© Tereshchenko Dmitry), 8 (© Loskutnikov), 10 (©
Foto- Ruhrgebiet), 13 (© Gridin), 14 (© tanewpix), 16
(LiteChoices ), 19 (© bioraven), 22 (©Hung Chung Chih
), 23 (© Trinh Le Nguyen), 27 (© Thomas Sztanek ), iii
(© Cristi180884), 15 (© Sukan ); The Art Archive p. 6
(Biblioteca Nacional Madrid/Gianni Dagli Orti ).

Cover photograph of bunch of colorful rubber bands
reproduced with permission of Photolibrary (Rubberball/
Mike Kemp).

We would like to thank Ann Fullick for her invaluable help
in the preparation of this book.

Every effort has been made to contact copyright holders of
any material reproduced in this book. Any omissions will
be rectified in subsequent printings if notice is given to the
publisher.

**Disclaimer**
All the Internet addresses (URLs) given in this book were
valid at the time of going to press. However, due to the
dynamic nature of the Internet, some addresses may have
changed, or sites may have changed or ceased to exist since
publication. While the author and publisher regret any
inconvenience this may cause readers, no responsibility for
any such changes can be accepted by either the author or
the publisher.

# Contents

Some words are shown in bold, **like this**.
You can find out what they mean by
looking in the glossary.

# Rubber in Our Lives

▲ The soles of these sneakers contain rubber.

Rubber is part of your everyday life. It is in the eraser you use to wipe away pencil marks. It is in the sneakers you wear. Rubber is in the balloon you blow up or the tennis ball you whack with a racket. Whether natural or **synthetic** (human-made), rubber in all forms is incredibly useful.

## Benefits of rubber

One benefit of rubber is that it stretches. We take advantage of that feature when we use rubber bands to hold papers or packages. **Latex** gloves, which are also made of rubber, stretch tightly over doctors' and nurses' hands. Rubber bandages stretch to the shape of knees and ankles to provide support for injured joints.

Rubber is waterproof. Rubber boots are a must for gardening, and rubber gloves keep hands dry when washing dishes. Scuba divers and surfers wear rubber suits, called wet suits, to keep cold water out and body heat in. Divers use masks with rubber seals to keep water off their faces, and they breathe through rubber hoses attached to air tanks.

Rubber bounces, and many sports would not exist without rubber balls. Basketballs and soccer balls have rubber linings that hold in air. Golf balls fly farther because of their rubber cores. Even bowling balls roll well because of rubber—although they do not bounce.

**Products with rubber**

The following products (and more) are made with rubber:

- balloons
- balls
- bandages
- bowling balls
- diving gear
- floor mats
- garden hoses
- latex gloves.

▼ **While most rubber balls bounce, this one knocks down bowling pins.**

# The History of Rubber

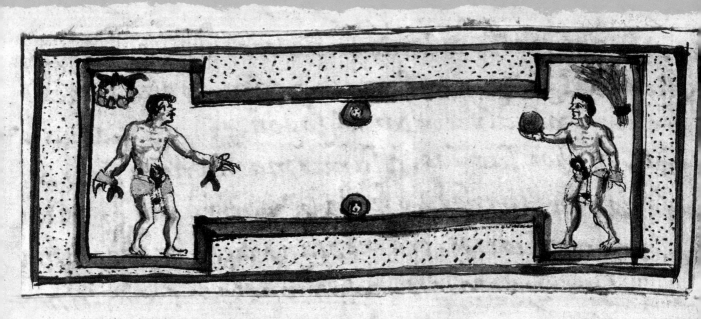

▲ These Aztec men are playing *ullama* with a rubber ball.

For centuries, the native people of South and Central America enjoyed the riches of their lands: gold, silver, and natural rubber. The Incas used rubber to coat the bottoms of their sandals, making the first waterproof shoes. Mayan priests offered food, gold, and rubber balls to the gods to gain their favor. The Aztecs made hollowed-out rubber statues.

The games *tlachtli* and *ullama* were a cross between basketball and football. The object of the game was to pass a rubber ball through a stone ring. The balls were about the size of a bowling ball. Most villages had courts for playing *tlachtli*. At times, conquering tribes made their captives play *tlachtli*. Mayan, Aztec, and Olmec warriors practiced their fighting skills by playing *tlachtli* or *ullama*.

# Rubber in Haiti

In 1493, when Italian explorer Christopher Columbus visited Haiti, he saw natives playing ball. Back in Europe he had seen carved wooden balls, but Haitian rubber balls bounced! The high-bouncing balls were made from a thick, milky liquid, which the natives collected from the *cau-uchu* tree. The rubber was **cured** over the smoke of burning palm nuts. Curing made the rubber solid.

Columbus brought some rubber balls back with him to Spain, but Europeans were more interested in gold and silver. Europeans did not realize that rubber could bring them riches. They only saw a child's toy. New uses for rubber would not come for many years.

◀ Christopher Columbus brought rubber balls back from the New World.

▲ Priestley's discovery has helped people erase millions of mistakes.

## Europeans and rubber

From 1492 to 1735, Europeans knew about rubber, but they were not interested in it. This began to change in 1735, when French scientist Charles de la Condamine studied rubber while on a trip to Peru.

Rubber was originally called *caoutchouc* from the native word "*cau-uchu*," which meant "weeping wood." This name described the way latex dripped from the bark of trees. Rubber got its name in 1770, when English scientist Joseph Priestley found that a wad of it was good at "rubbing out" pencil marks on paper. Pencil erasers were among the first uses Europeans had for rubber.

## Uses for rubber increase

In 1820 sailors who traveled to Brazil saw people wearing shoes with rubber-covered soles. One person took 500 pairs of these shoes back to Boston, Massachusetts. Boston's rainy weather made waterproof shoes valuable, and one clever merchant got rich.

A short time later, in 1823, Scottish chemist Charles Macintosh developed a way to coat cloth with rubber. Macintosh made waterproof fabrics by placing a thin layer of rubber between two layers of wool. Today, people in the United Kingdom call raincoats "Macintoshes" after Charles Macintosh.

Rubber had limits, as it melted if it got too hot and shattered if it got too cold. In 1839 U.S. inventor Charles Goodyear fixed this problem. He discovered the process of **vulcanization** by adding **sulfur** to rubber and heating it. Vulcanized rubber was stronger, more useful, and perfect for making another invention—rubber tires. Over the next 50 years, scientists developed dozens of new rubber products.

▼ **In the late 1800s, bicycles like these had thin rubber tires.**

▲ Today, rubber bands come in a variety of sizes and colors.

## New uses for rubber

Englishman Stephen Perry developed the first rubber bands in 1845. Perry used rubber bands to hold papers and envelopes together. The rubber was manufactured using Goodyear's vulcanization process.

Inventors continued to experiment with rubber. In 1852 American Hiram Hutchinson got the rights to use Goodyear's rubber to create rain boots called Wellington boots. The boots were named for the Duke of Wellington, a great English military leader.

**Chicle** ✓

Ancient Mayans and Aztecs collected *chicle*, a rubber-like sap from the sapodilla tree, and chewed it like gum.

In 1869 American William Finley Semple received the first **patent** (meaning he received exclusive rights to make it) for chewing gum. In 1871 U.S. inventor Thomas Adams received a **patent** for the chewing gum we know today. About 25 years later, doctors at Johns Hopkins in Baltimore, Maryland, began wearing rubber gloves during surgery. One-piece rubber golf balls were made popular in 1898 by an Ohio golfer named Coburn Haskell.

# Rubber in the early 1900s

In the early 1900s, electricity replaced gas and coal as a power source. Wires carried electricity from power plants to lights, heating coils, and stoves. While electricity brought many benefits, it also brought the dangers of electric shock and fires. Rubber **insulation** protected people from these dangers.

The use of automobiles rose during the early 1900s. Rubber played an important role, as cars ran on rubber tires and had rubber horns.

In 1928 Fleer produced the first bubble gum. Chewing gum originally contained *chicle*, a different type of rubber from the rubber used in insulation or tires. Fleer sold more than $1.5 million worth of gum in the first year.

◀ One of the most exciting rubber inventions was stretchy pink bubble gum.

▲ Creating tanks like these required a lot of rubber.

## Synthetic rubber and war

During World War I (1914–18), people became interested in developing synthetic rubber. Rubber came from South America and Southeast Asia, but during the war many ships sank at sea. So, people wanted a way to make their own rubber. In 1930 the DuPont Company developed the first workable synthetic rubber, called **neoprene**.

During World War II (1939–45), the Allies (the United Kingdom, France, the United States, Canada, Russia, and more than a dozen other nations) fought against the Axis powers (led by Germany, Italy, and Japan). By 1941 Germany and Japan controlled 95 percent of the world's natural rubber supply.

The Allies were desperate for rubber for their equipment. Every large tank, called a Sherman tank, used 450 kilograms (992 pounds) of rubber. Warships had more than 20,000 rubber parts. In 1941 chemical companies in the United States made about 8,000 tons of synthetic rubber.

## Health uses

Viruses and bacteria cannot pass through rubber, so rubber helps prevent the spread of disease. In the late 1900s, health concerns made wearing latex gloves required for workers who dealt with people or food. Latex gloves protect both the workers and the people they serve.

## Rubber today

Scientists continue to find new uses for rubber. In 2010 engineers at Princeton University, in New Jersey, invented rubber sheets that produce electricity. When the rubber sheets are attached to running shoes, a runner's jogging can generate enough energy to power a cell phone.

**Synthetic becomes standard**

Today, more synthetic rubber is used each year than natural rubber.

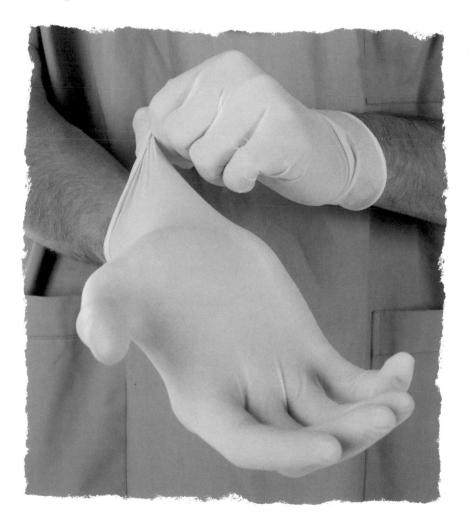

◄ Latex gloves protect people from infections.

# Growing and Making Rubber

▲ **Plantations use small pails for collecting latex.**

Rubber trees need a hot, wet climate. Several types of rubber trees grow wild in Central and South America. Ninety percent of natural latex rubber comes from the *Hevea* rubber tree. In Brazil, *Hevea* trees grow wild throughout the Amazon River Basin. Guayule, a plant from the sunflower family, grows in the dry desert regions of Mexico and the southwestern United States. Latex from guayule is a lot like latex from the *Hevea* tree. *Chicle*, another natural rubber, comes from the sapodilla tree. (*Chicle*, however, does not make hard rubber when vulcanized.)

## From Brazil to Southeast Asia

In the 1800s, Brazil controlled the rubber industry. The owners of large farms called **plantations** made millions of dollars, and Manaus, Brazil, became the center of their business. Plantation owners lived like kings. Their wives wore diamonds and fine silks. The workers, on the other hand, were paid very little money, lived in shacks, and had barely enough food to survive. Workers had no schools or doctors. At that time, no other country produced rubber.

In 1876 British explorer Henry Wickham secretly collected 70,000 rubber tree seeds in Brazil and brought them to London. He used the seeds to start rubber plantations in Africa, Sri Lanka, and Singapore. By the 1920s, most rubber production had shifted from Brazil to Asia.

▼ **Rubber trees in Asian plantations are planted in even rows to make collecting the latex easier.**

## How rubber is made

Collecting latex from rubber trees is hard work. The
process is called **tapping**, and the workers are tappers.
A tapper makes cuts into the bark of the rubber tree at
an angle. The sap, called latex, drips into a bucket that
hangs below the cut. Workers collect the buckets and
take them to be **processed**.

A single rubber tree gives about 236 milliliters
(8 ounces) of latex in three hours. The cut slowly seals
itself after three hours, and a new cut must be made.
Cuts cannot be too deep, or they will kill the trees.
If cuts are too shallow, the sap will not run. Only an
expert tapper is allowed to cut rubber trees.

# Processing latex

Every few hours, workers bring pails of latex to a
central collection area. The latex is white, thick, and
gooey, like honey. It hardens when it comes into
contact with air. Workers mix the liquid rubber with
a chemical substance, such as **ammonia**. The chemicals
keep the latex liquid. The latex is then sealed in large
containers for shipping to a processing plant. If
the latex does harden, the solid blocks can later
be dissolved.

At a rubber processing plant, most rubber is vulcanized.
Latex, sulfur, and other chemicals are mixed together
and then heated. **Carbon** may be added to make the
rubber black. Vulcanized rubber is used for tires, seals
on machines, medical instruments, hoses, and hundreds
of other products. It is long lasting, strong, and easy to
work with.

◀ Liquid latex is
mixed with chemical
substances so it does
not harden.

# Uses for Rubber

▶ **Fourteen percent of a car tire is natural rubber. Twenty-seven percent is synthetic rubber.**

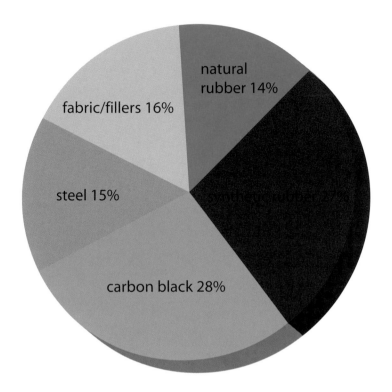

natural rubber 14%

fabric/fillers 16%

steel 15%

synthetic rubber 27%

carbon black 28%

## Uses for Rubber

Natural and synthetic rubbers have several properties that make rubber a useful material. Rubber provides insulation against heat or electric current. It is strong, flexible, and lasts a long time. It is waterproof, so it keeps materials and people dry.

Some rubber is poured into shaped **molds** to make products such as tires, fishing lures, or toys. For products such as latex gloves, rubber needs to be thin. Molds are dipped into latex, cooled, and peeled off the forms. Rubber can be made into thread and woven into fabric to make **elastic** bands, like those found in underwear.

## Long wearing

More than half the natural rubber produced each year is used to make tires. Every tire has half as much natural rubber as synthetic rubber. Large tires, such as those made for earthmoving equipment, can contain 2,903 kilograms (6,400 pounds) of rubber. The mix of natural and synthetic rubbers builds stronger tires.

This strength makes rubber perfect for use in different kinds of manufacturing, as parts made of rubber can withstand wear and tear. Rubber is used to produce smooth-running **conveyor belts** in factories and to line storage tanks and railroad cars.

## Flexible

Rubber stretches and bounces back into shape, as seen in rubber bands and balloons. The ability to stretch also makes latex paint roll on more smoothly, and it allows foam mattresses to conform to the shape of our bodies.

▼ Latex balloons stretch as they are blown up.

▲ Rubber makes it easier to play on this tennis court.

## Sports

Rubber is long lasting, waterproof, and can be either soft and flexible or very hard. These characteristics make rubber great for sports equipment. Because rubber bounces, the balls we play with contain at least some rubber. Rubber in sports shoes prevents slipping on floors or grass. We shoot hard, black rubber hockey pucks at goals or roll rubber bowling balls down lanes. Rubber floors provide softer, safer places for athletes who play basketball, tennis, and volleyball. The rubber used in these cases is vulcanized rubber.

## Protection and insulation

Many liquids and gases cannot pass through rubber. That is the reason rubber is used for hoses and tubing in cars, hospitals, gardens, and gas stations.

Rubber-coated coats and hats protect us from foul weather. Gardeners, fishers, and firefighters wear rubber boots to keep their feet dry.

### Earthquake protection

In Japan, more than 2,500 buildings have rubber **bearings** to protect them from earthquake damage. Bearings are round balls that support machinery. The bearings make the buildings "flexible" so that they can withstand a quake and not fall apart.

Rubber offers insulation that keeps warmth or coolness in. Wet suits made from synthetic rubber allow divers to travel deep into cold waters and still stay warm. Rubber weather strips prevent heat from escaping from a building.

Rubber also provides the kind of insulation that protects again the flow of electricity. Rubber insulation guards against electric shocks. Rubber is wrapped around electric wires or cords. It is also used for producing electrical outlet boxes and switches.

▼ **Rubber boots keep feet dry in the rain.**

# Rubber and the Environment

▲ When people clear forest to plant a rubber plantation, it may destroy the habitat of giant pandas.

Rubber plantations create serious problems for the **environment**. Rubber-growing countries cut down natural forests to make room for bigger rubber plantations. They destroy the **habitats** of plants and animals. In areas such as Indonesia, India, and China, this destruction is particularly dangerous for **endangered species** such as Sumatran tigers, Sumatran rhinos, orangutans, and giant pandas. Those species are close to becoming **extinct**, or dying out.

Loss of native plants also increases soil **erosion**, a process through which soil is gradually worn away. Rubber plants do not stop wind or water from washing away soil. It also causes water **pollution** because some latex drips into the soil when trees are trapped.

# Pollution

Rubber-processing factories produce several environmental problems, including pollution. Vulcanizing rubber uses chemical **compounds**, such as lead and zinc oxide. These chemicals are poisonous, and the poisoned waste liquid gets into soil or flows into rivers, streams, and lakes. The poison in bodies of water kills the fish and animals that drink the water. It also poisons humans, who need local water for drinking, cooking, and bathing. The amount of chemical waste from processing rubber is at least 25 times greater than the amount of rubber produced.

**Deforestation** is the loss of forests by cutting down trees. Most deforestation comes from clearing land to plant more rubber trees. This destroys habitats and reduces the amount of food for animals that live in the forests. Native plant eaters, such as pandas and rhinos, do not eat rubber plants. The soil suffers as well, washing away in the heavy rains that come yearly in Southeast Asia.

▼ **Deforestation harms the environment.**

▲ Ground-up tires produce a variety of different flooring products.

## Why recycle?

Rubber creates large amounts of trash, but it does not rot like an apple that is thrown away. No living things feed on processed rubber. A tire in a **landfill** takes thousands of years to decay. Tires also fill with gas and float to the surface of a landfill.

The good news is that rubber can be **recycled**. Recycling rubber saves resources, energy, and money. Rubber from recycling costs half as much as natural or synthetic rubber that has never been used. Producing 450 grams (1 pound) of recycled rubber requires only 29 percent of the energy needed to make the same amount of new rubber.

The main source of recycled rubber is tires. The quickest way to recycle a tire is to have new **tread** (grooves) put on it. While many large vehicle tires, such as those for trucks, are retread, most car tires are not. The **European Union (EU)** has set a goal to retread one-quarter of all car tires.

## Products of rubber recycling

Grinding up rubber tires into crumbs produces a product that can be used in many ways. Rubber crumb is added to asphalt, the material used to make roads. It makes good mulch, a protective ground covering left around plants. The crumb can be processed into new tires, roofing materials, floor tiles, and floor mats.

**Tennis, anyone?**

In 2001 a **conservation** group found a way to recycle the used balls from the Wimbledon tennis tournament. The balls make excellent homes for endangered harvest mice.

▼ **The rubber lining in this tennis ball keeps this harvest mouse's home waterproof.**

# Today's Rubber Market

CHINA

India

Thailand

Vietnam

PHILIPPINES

Sri Lanka

Malaysia

INDONESIA

▲ **These countries in Southeast Asia are major rubber producers.**

Rubber is like any other crop. Too much or too little rain, severe temperature changes, and bad storms affect rubber trees. Trees younger than seven years old cannot be tapped, and trees older than 32 years old produce very little latex.

The countries that produce the most natural rubber are Thailand, Indonesia, Malaysia, India, and Vietnam. Although India and Malaysia also process rubber, other major growers ship most of their product elsewhere.

As of 2003, China became the largest user of natural rubber. Most of China's natural rubber is used in making tires. India and the United States also manufacture more rubber products than any other nations. Malaysia, where rubber trees grow and rubber is processed, also makes many rubber products.

In 2009 India, China, and Malaysia, combined, used about 47 percent of the world's natural rubber. The supply of natural rubber is not keeping pace with the demand. To keep the supply steady, farmers need to replace old rubber trees and begin collecting rubber from trees planted seven years earlier.

## Part of our world

We make and use hundreds of rubber products in our daily lives, from gigantic earthmover tires to stretchy rubber bands. With increased demand comes the need to find ways to reduce pollution and waste. What a change from Christopher Columbus's time, when rubber's main use was making balls for games!

▼ **Earthmover tires are made of 2,903 kilograms (6,400 pounds) of rubber!**

# Timeline

(These dates are often approximations.)

**1600 BCE**
The Mayan people make balls from natural rubber.

0

**1600**

**1735**
French scientist Charles de la Condamine studies rubber, which he learns about in Peru.

**1770**
John Priestley finds that natural rubber "rubs away" pencil marks and calls the substance "rubber."

**1700**

**1869**
The first patent for chewing gum is issued to William Finley Semple.

**1848**
Rubber golf balls are introduced by the Reverend Adam Paterson, in St. Andrews, Scotland.

**1876**
Sir Henry Wickham collects some 70,000 rubber tree seeds and secretly carries them back to London from Brazil.

**1894**
Doctors at Johns Hopkins begin wearing latex gloves during surgery.

**1898**
The one-piece rubber golf ball becomes popular.

**1950s**
People use rubber flooring for the first time.

**1980s**
Latex gloves become standard for use in all medical facilities.

⋀⋀⋀ This symbol shows where there is a change of scale in the timeline or where a long period of time with no noted events has been left out.

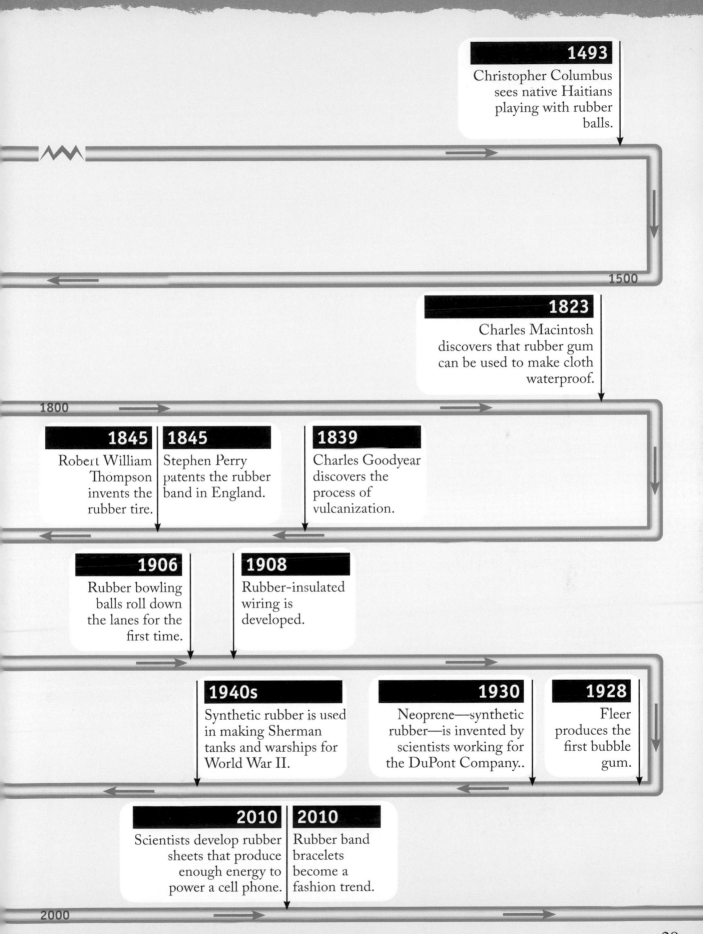

**1493**
Christopher Columbus sees native Haitians playing with rubber balls.

1500

**1823**
Charles Macintosh discovers that rubber gum can be used to make cloth waterproof.

1800

**1845**
Robert William Thompson invents the rubber tire.

**1845**
Stephen Perry patents the rubber band in England.

**1839**
Charles Goodyear discovers the process of vulcanization.

**1906**
Rubber bowling balls roll down the lanes for the first time.

**1908**
Rubber-insulated wiring is developed.

**1940s**
Synthetic rubber is used in making Sherman tanks and warships for World War II.

**1930**
Neoprene—synthetic rubber—is invented by scientists working for the DuPont Company..

**1928**
Fleer produces the first bubble gum.

**2010**
Scientists develop rubber sheets that produce enough energy to power a cell phone.

**2010**
Rubber band bracelets become a fashion trend.

2000

# Glossary

**ammonia** colorless, strong chemical compound of nitrogen and hydrogen

**bearing** round ball that supports, guides, or supports machinery

**carbon** common non-metallic element

*chicle* natural rubber sap used for chewing gum

**compound** mixture made of two or more chemical elements

**conservation** act of preserving something

**conveyor belt** endless surface that rolls along and carries items on it—for example, in a factory

**cured** preserved by heating

**deforestation** act of clear-cutting a forest

**elastic** type of rubber that is capable of being stretched or expanded

**endangered species** animal or plant species (group of living things) that is in danger of no longer existing

**environment** air, water, minerals, and living things in an area

**erosion** process of being worn away by water, air, or chemicals

**European Union** association of countries in Europe, formed in 1993

**extinct** having no living members

**habitat** natural environment of a living thing

**insulation** material used to keep heat or cold in, or to protect against the flow of electricity

**landfill** area with buried waste materials

**latex** milky liquid that is processed into rubber

**mold** container for making a shape

**neoprene** oil-resistant synthetic rubber used in paint, shoe soles, and wet suits

**patent** government license that gives the holder exclusive rights to make a product

**plantation** large farm that grows one main crop

**pollution** act of introducing harmful substances into the air, water, or soil

**process** actions for doing something

**recycle** renew, reuse, or process for another use

**sulfur** yellow, non-metallic element

**synthetic** made by humans, not nature

**tapping** cutting trees to allow natural latex to ooze out

**tread** tire grooves

**vulcanization** act of mixing latex with chemicals and heating it to make rubber harder, stronger, and more long lasting

# Find Out More

## Books

Gleason, Carrie. *The Biography of Rubber (How Did That Get Here?)*. New York: Crabtree, 2006.

Thomson, Ruth. *Rubber (Recycling and Reusing)*. Mankato, Minn.: Smart Apple Media, 2006.

## Websites

The Guardians: Natural Rubber Industry
**www.theguardians.com/rainforest/htmlsite/factfile/rubber.htm**
Read dozens of facts about rubber and rubber trees at this website.

University of Wisconsin: Rubber Trees
**www.uwec.edu/geography/Ivogeler/w111/rubber.htm**
Find out more about rubber trees at this website.

Goodyear: How to Make a Tire
**www.goodyear.ca/tire_school/howtomake.html**
How do you make a tire? Find out here!

Candy Favorites: A Brief History of Chewing Gum
**www.candyfavorites.com/shop/catalog-gum-history.php**
Discover how rubber became chewing gum.

# Index